Y0-BBD-427

Between the Lakes:

The Poets of Linden Hills

ISBN 0-9777915-0-5

First printing        March 2006


published by Trolley Car Press
printed by Sentinel Printing
250 North Highway 10, St. Cloud, MN 56304

Additional copies of this book may be ordered by mail:
Send $14.95, plus $5 for shipping and handling, to

Trolley Car Press
3019 West 43$^{rd}$ Street
Minneapolis, MN 55410

For multiple-copy discounts, contact Doug Wilhide,
612-926-3939, or wilhide@skypoint.com

To order online, contact
The Bibelot
www.bibelotshops.com


Some of the poetry included in this book has
been published previously in other books and in various journals,
magazines and newspapers. All poems are used
with permission of the authors.


Cover photographs by Doug Wilhide.
Front: Lake Harriet with runners
Back: Linden Hills trolley station

**Profits from this book will be used to benefit
Linden Hills poetry programs and the poets included here.**

For Jean, Sam and Anduin, who make it all both possible and worthwhile.

## Acknowledgments

A book like this is really a kind of poem itself, celebrating lots of people who help make a community. It wouldn't have happened, of course, without the collaboration of the poets included, but it wouldn't have been conceived without the many other poets and writers who live in Linden Hills.

The Linden Hills Neighborhood Council (LHINC) has been a key force in the effort to make poetry more prominent in the neighborhood. For a while we had a "poetry committee" who supported my efforts as Poet Laureate of Linden Hills -- Sylvia Fine, Leonard Lang and, especially, Susan Perry, who first came up with the idea of having a neighborhood Poet Laureate. Jack Jaglo, as a leader of LHINC, was the person who suggested I apply. Actually he said, "You have to do this." His wife, Chris, taught math to our kids. I've learned to do whatever they tell me to. Rae Ann Vandeputte has been a great asset, helping to publicize our efforts on the LHINC website. Felicity Britton has been a wonderful supporter (as well as a talented poet). She was the one who said, "Why don't you do a book?"

Thanks also go to the many people who have attended or hosted "salons" and supported neighborhood poetry events: Patty and Rick Dietz, Kris Mortensen, Felicity Britton, George Scott, Carrie Bassett, Black Eyed Susan's gift shop, the Bibelot, Great Harvest Bakery, Dunn Brothers and Rag and Bone Books (now departed but sorely missed). I'd also like to thank Steve Wright and his eager fifth graders at Carondelet School and John Dunham at Southwest High School for inviting me into their classrooms.

Finally I must thank my family: my wife, Jean, my son, Sam, and my daughter, Anduin. They have endured my enthusiasm for poetry, attended events, supported all the effort required to produce this book, and tried not to roll their eyes when someone refers to me as a "poet laureate."

Doug Wilhide

# Contents

# Put your money into poetry

Spend! Feed your poets!
Spend! See to their happiness!
Give them meaning and comfort
Give them shelter and warmth
Give them money and laughter and support
Give them plenty to drink!

The world will little note nor long remember
What you do here, or what you think
But your poets grant you permission
To capture love and loss and beauty,
So you can outlive faith, even religion.
Spend! Do your duty!

Spend! Convince your committees!
Your minutes and your meetings are passing fancies.
Who remembers last year's crises?
The pros and cons, the budgets and prices --
They are passing as snowmen and manners.
Where are the monuments to planners?

Invest in your poets, support their art:
They are your mutual funds for eternity.
But even poets need to eat, so spend! Do your part,
Measure returns in lives led fully.
Open your hearts! Empty your pockets! Offer your best!
Ars longa, vita brevis est!

# Introduction

Who cares about poetry any more?  It seems, somehow, so
unnecessary, so out of the mainstream, so tangential to our
lives.  If we think of poetry at all we usually think in terms of
rhyming lines or the poems we had to write in school.  Some of
us, maybe, kept writing a little longer until we grew up and
went on to more everyday pursuits.

If we meet someone now who calls himself or herself "a poet,"
we wince.  What kind of pretentious nonsense is this?  What do
you really do for a living?  Would I have read any of your books?
Why don't you write novels instead?

And yet, and yet, and yet...

It wasn't always this way.  Those of us who went to college in or
around the 1960s thought of poetry differently.  Many of us
studied the liberal arts, and even business and professional
schools back then required students to be exposed to a "core
curriculum" that included plays, novels, essays and poems.  A
surprisingly large number of us became English majors.

Back in those days, poetry seemed more important.  Poets, too.
In our mid-century struggle to find meaning and "relevance,"
we read poetry as if it were a kind of religion and looked to
poets as stand-ins for pastors and priests.

Homer was our original intelligent designer and "The Odyssey"
and "The Iliad" were the texts (we were taught) from which all

2

civilization derived. We met Shakespeare on his own ground and, in countless "modern" productions, on ours. We read Whitman's "Leaves of Grass" both for the sexy parts and the ideas that formed the basis (we were taught) of a real American literature. On mid-twentieth century college campuses, e.e. cummings, William Carlos Williams and other Imagists were fun, quick reads. Robert Frost was stopping by woods and choosing a path not taken -- and looked the part of a poet. Dylan Thomas sounded like one. Auden was supposed to be a great one. Sylvia Plath a doomed one. Jack Kerouac was our prodigal son role model. Ferlinghetti was where we wanted to be. Wallace Stevens was our sage in a gray flannel suit. T.S. Eliot was the voice of God.

And it wasn't just on college campuses where poetry and poets held authority. I worked in construction one summer and still recall hauling bricks for a mason who could recite, flawlessly and completely, Robert Service's "The Cremation of Sam McGee." Our parents all seemed to know at least one poem by Longfellow or Tennyson or Wordsworth. Grandparents could recite parts of "Paul Revere's Ride" or the story of the village blacksmith under the spreading chestnut tree. Everyone knew that only God (not T.S. Eliot) could make a tree.

So when did it all change? What pushed poetry so far into the background? The last half century has not been especially kind to the special writing that poetry is. We have grown used to getting our stories, images and meaning from novels, television, movies, advertising, magazines and, more recently, from video games, email and blogs. If it isn't visual, sensational or short it doesn't matter. Some of us have even gone back to church.

And yet, and yet, and yet...

Poetry is still around. We just encounter it in more limited circumstances. Our children (and in some cases, our grandchildren) go to school and read poetry and write their own poems. We put them up on refrigerators with magnets that can be arranged to make other poems. When someone gets married we read a poem. When someone dies we read a poem. Young kids are into Shel Silverstein and recite their own versions of nursery rhymes. The internet is alive with web pages devoted to poets and poems.

We have had some accessible U.S. Poets Laureate recently. They may not reach all of us, but they try. Rita Dove writes technically refined poetry of African-American life, telling stories of everything from Caribbean slaves to ballroom dancing. Billy Collins writes deceptively simple poetry about everyday events that makes us laugh and think and say "I know just what he means." Ted Kooser, a Nebraskan, writes engaging verse that gets to the heart of modern, midwestern experience.

And in neighborhoods around the country you'll find poets lurking – less well known, perhaps, but every bit as enjoyable.

Linden Hills, a small area within the city limits of Minneapolis, is one of those neighborhoods. It's a beautiful place, tucked between two lakes: Calhoun to the north and Harriet to the east. The "hills" aren't much, mostly a series of small rises that lead up and down to the lakes. The linden trees have been hit

4

hard recently by disease and summer storms, but there are still enough of them to characterize the community.

In summer the lindens, oaks, maples and some surviving elms arch over the streets and form a canopy. When the sunlight streams through, it's like walking through a cathedral. In the fall the trees turn color and the whole place lights up with yellows and reds and oranges, framing the deep blue of the lakes. In winter the evergreens take precedence. We get snow, the lakes freeze, people skate, and the place looks like something out of a Currier and Ives drawing. In the spring cherry and apple trees bloom and compete in color with gardens of tulips and daffodils.

Linden Hills is a kind of village within the city. A lot of the homes were built 80-100 years ago as summer cottages for people who lived in "downtown" Minneapolis. There was another big building boom in the 1950s and 60s -- small homes that were then expanded because people don't want to move. We have at least two shopping districts that host an eclectic variety of stores, restaurants and coffee shops. It's not especially "upscale," but it is convenient. I can bike or drive downtown in about twenty minutes, walk to get groceries, coffee, lunch or dinner, ice cream, a bagel or a can of paint.

The lakes, of course, are the main attraction. Calhoun is slightly larger and more urban. It borders on Uptown, which is a larger shopping area and the preferred docking port for generations of young people moving out of the house and into a first apartment. Harriet is more residential, smaller and quieter. Migrating birds stop here twice a year: lots of gulls and coots and Canadian geese. I have seen loons, bald eagles, herons and, once, a flock of trumpeter swans. Both lakes are home tracks to walkers, bikers and joggers -- at all hours and in all seasons. A survey a few years ago asked people what they did around the lakes. The most frequent answer was "think."

A lot of writers live here. We have novelists, playwrights, essayists and journalists, advertising copywriters and writers of children's books. And we have poets. We even have our own Poet Laureate. At the moment, it's me. The program was started in 2003 by the Linden Hills Neighborhood Council as a way to use poetry to help bring neighbors together. Since my appointment, we've hosted public readings, a poetry slam, guest talks in local schools and a series of "salons" where we get together with food, wine and a theme and read our favorite poetry.

The poems included here have been written by poets who live in, or have close ties to, Linden Hills. But it's not just local poetry. The themes range from love and loss to farting. The forms range from limericks and sonnets to ballads and free verse. The locations range from Australia to around the corner. Some of the poems have been published previously, some appear here for the first time.

Many of these poets have wide experience and deep understanding, as well as a commitment to poetry. A few examples: George Scott is in his 70s and an expert limericist. He uses the form for humor but also explores the meaning of everyday life. Stephan GrandPré is a college student. Esam Aal writes short poems from the perspective of a Muslim living in America. Felicity Britton is a transplanted Aussie who writes poetry about the struggles of love and loneliness and raising kids. Kirsten Bergh, a talented young poet, died in a tragic traffic accident several years ago. She was 17.

The selection is my responsibility, for better or worse. I've tried to choose poems that have some kind of edge to them and show off a distinctive voice. I've also tried to include a wide variety. Some are easy reads, some require a little more attention. Some will make you laugh, some will make you think, some will break your heart, some will give you hope.

I know there are other poets living in Linden Hills, and other poetry that deserves to be read and enjoyed, but this is what I've come in contact with and what my ear tells me is good.

I hope you'll agree. If so, perhaps we'll have another volume in the future.

Enjoy!

Doug Wilhide
Minneapolis, January 2006

## Doug Wilhide

*I've written poetry for as long as I can remember.  It just seems like a natural thing to do, and since I'm a life-long English major I walk around with lines of famous poems in my head. Sometimes my poems sort of happen -- a couple lines, a rhyme or a bit of rhythm -- and I just try to get them down before they disappear.*

*I grew up in a small town in the South, longing for something more open and free.  The suburbs weren't the answer.  Linden Hills offers the best balance I've found.  City enough to offer variety and sophistication, village enough to be a real community.  It's also beautiful.  It feels like home.*

# Linden Hills

Two people sat in the public place
On a bench, under the maple trees
where the buses come and the people go
Two people sat quietly.

The place was laid with old brick and seemed old
But it wasn't. The brick was salvaged, the benches aged --
The space was designed to look old --
And it took three tries before the trees survived.

The two people were honestly old
having lived together through hard times, good times,
happiness, tragedies, trips to far off places, children,
victories, defeats, house cleanings and evenings with wine.

Two people sat together under a sky threatening rain
Not talking much, laughing once or twice,
Just sat there, then got up and walked away,
Half in the place, half in the past, half in tomorrow.

Those old people you sometimes see
Sitting there -- my love: that was you and me.

# The Family

She talks to the cat more than she should.
They can't be good for each other --
her engagement with life's nuances
his awful cynicism.

.

He's a ferocious old fart
Though he can't hear and he can't talk.
He sees a world full of fools
and is not shy about his grievances.

She's allergic to cats
And into life's small facts.
She organizes like an undertaker
but it's winter and one makes allowances.

Both of them are now past fifty.
They can be as weird as they want to be.

# My Glacier

My driveway is a glacier that
melts and freezes, melts and freezes and
creeps dangerously through a slow winter.

I have tried everything: snowblowing, shovelling,
salt, sawdust, ice chopping and chicken grit,
but my glacier retains its slick, menacing momentum.

Global warming is no problem for this ice flow
that threatens the postman, the pizza guy,
my friends and my aging, at-risk bones.

We challenge gravity along its glassy surface.
We take smaller and ever-smaller steps and
-- fearing every slip -- glide down like penguins disembarking.

Come April (or maybe May) the ice will melt and
our strides will lengthen, our balance return.
Our memories of this cold, dark, ice age will diminish.

But until then the Great Driveway Glacier awaits:
a saber-toothed beast of a thing
anticipating the next -- and possibly final -- fall.

# Winter Geese Near Lake Calhoun

In the snow falling, slush freezing,
winter whitening morning
they are there where they should not be,
Clustered, in pairs or wandering alone --
by the lake side
by the ice side
beside the beautiful lake.

Did someone miss the memo?
Hey!  It's below below out here and heading south
which is what you guys should have done months ago.
Hey!  You listening to me?
There's a margarita with my name on it
where you should be:
bird dummies.

They are, in their own way, their own work of art:
"study in black and white and warm grey."
They are elegant definers of a world and a way;
they could be Parisian gentlemen at a cafe
or dancers resting before a play.

We are out of step, these birds and I,
unable to follow simple directions or ancient rhythms,
convinced in spite of all the evidence we are right
and ready to endure, even enjoy, the consequences.

While others opt for comfort and a place much more forgiving
Getting through a winter is, for us, a living.

# Just Before Winter

The old lady in the baggy sweater
(both of them grey as November)
raked leaves into small piles in the street.
That morning, alone with her coffee, she had read the notice:
DO NOT RAKE LEAVES INTO THE STREET.

Harrumphing, she had taken a sip of coffee
and, thinking about a cigarette,
suddenly remembered the smell of burning leaves
when she was young and you could still do that in the city.

All day the memory had stayed with her
vivid as a year's first snowfall or an evening's first martini.
She felt the scratch of a plaid wool skirt
she had worn one warm, fall football day,
Recalled the taste of cool apple cider washing down
Nut and berry breads fresh from the oven,
Remembered running unfettered, hair blowing in her eyes,
through a field of hay bales and pumpkins.

Late in the evening as a pre-snow drizzle turned colder,
the old lady put on her grey, baggy sweater,
and escorted her arthritis out the door.
She took a rake, a broom and a dustpan to the front yard
and began to clear her leaves.

14

There weren't many and they weren't hers:
mostly blown over from the neighbors' maple
when he fired up his goddam noisy leaf blower --
Leftovers really, like her --
but she attended to them anyway,
stopping often to rest,
achingly fulfilling civic obligations.

She raked them into the street and meticulously
arranged them into dustpan-sized piles.
When I passed she was sweeping them up, one at a time,
bent over, swearing softly, pissed off and
at peace with the world.

## John's Wolf

The wolf that died...
the big one with the yellow eyes
the original nightmare that went bump in the night
the evil on four legs with breath you could hear and smell...

The huge wolf --
even in daylight bigger than hope and comfort and love --
after dark, monstrous and inescapable
sticky as blood, with claws like razors, matted fur,
   teeth like scythes...

The wolf of worse-than-death,
slobbering, terrible, fast as fear,
the killing machine, cold beyond reason, beyond prayer...
the enormous wolf that died...

Last night it followed me home.

# Hope

and there it was, the white-sailed boat

so unexpected

so central to everything,

with the lake blowing up blue water

the grey-dark clouds in the eastern sky

and the trees nearly neon with color,

caught in the act of autumn

by the searchlight of the sun.

# Today I Will Not Be Old

Today I will not be old...
I will not feel the pain in my knees.
If I have to push to get up from sitting or kneeling,
I will do it without making noise.

Today I will not be old...
I will not criticize the young for their ignorance or ineptitude.
I will admire them for their grace, their beauty and their
joy in encountering the world afresh.

Today I will not be old...
I will not judge experiences that seem less interesting
                    than those of my youth.
I will not say, "Oh, I have seen a bigger one of those,
a finer example of that, or a better one of these."

Today I will not be old...
If I am praised I will not deny it, but will revel in it
                    and be as vain as I please.
I will look for honest ways to praise others
and will overlook their failings and forgive my own.

Today I will not be old...
I will believe I can walk as far as I want
                    and carry whatever I need.
If my back aches, I will rest and enjoy the easing of pain,
but I will not rest over long.

18

Today I will not be old...
I will notice and rejoice at the laughter of children
And not be annoyed by their inconvenience
or saddened by the disappointments they may encounter.

Today I will not be old...
I will not build conversation around illness or disease,
either my own or those of my peers, relatives or friends.
I will talk about the joys of new things encountered.

Today I will not be old...
I will not summarize. I will respect the nuances
          of each encounter.
I will look at change carefully and not conclude that it
is always for the worse.

Today I will not be old...
(...a work in progress...)

19

## self portrait

dances with words
dallies with semi-colons
plays with periods and
commits to commas

this is the writer
perched in his mind
working to find
the Northwest passage
the new found land
the Panama that links
the out of us to the in

parcing psychologies
hustling history
selecting from selves
he steers by the light of
the heart.

# Wave bouncing: directions

First find a shallow beach
in the summer
or in one of those places
where summer always is.

Then find a wave
breaking, but not too much
one of a long line of waves
with an appropriate pedigree.

Wade out so your toes just touch
and as each wave comes
tap lightly on the sand beneath your feet
and let the wave carry you
up and over.

Do this again and again
until you are tired of it
or gravity pulls you
back to shore.

# The daughter who wouldn't get out of her bed

The daughter who wouldn't get out of her bed
Had toes on her feet and hair on her head
"I'm much like other daughters," she said,
"It's just that I don't want to get out of bed."

Her mother pleaded. "Please get up," she said.
But the daughter who wouldn't get out of her bed
Purred like a cat who's been very well fed
And sank deeper into her covers instead.

"You know," said the Mom, "there are books to be read
Flowers to smell, hikes to be led,
Clothes to be shopped for and music," she said
To the daughter who wouldn't get out of her bed.

"What will happen?" her poor mother said,
"You'll miss school and miss parties; you never will wed."
But the daughter who wouldn't get out of her bed
Smiled sweetly and pulled the blanket up over her head.

Then the father came home and in a Dad voice he said
To the daughter who wouldn't get out of her bed:
"I love you my darling, but don't be mislead,
You must get up and get going if you want to be fed."

"Oh," said the daughter who wouldn't get out of her bed,
"Perhaps you can fetch me some food -- dear, kind old Dad --
Strawberries are nice, with some cream and short bread,
I'm comfy and you're so already up and about instead."

Now sometimes this story makes parents see red
And sometimes the young folks bring wrath on my head
But this is the truth, the whole truth as I've said
About the daughter who wouldn't get out of her bed.

# Earleye in the Morning

I fell in love with a gypsy girl
Who said she'd be my woman;
I took her to bed one night in May
And went no more a roaming.
Her hair was dark, her legs were long
Her eyes were grey as rivers;
She asked me if I'd stay with her
I said I'd stay forever

We danced away the summer days
from night 'till earleye morning
But then the leaves began to turn
And me, I felt like roaming.
I left her one October night
When autumn winds were blowing
And now it seems I've spent my life
Out on the seas a'sailing.

I know the way the sea winds blow,
I know the lands they blow to,
But if I had my choice again
There's just one land I'd go to:
I'm going to the forest where
For once I wasn't roaming,
I'm going to leave the sea someday
And follow my gypsy woman.

(based on the traditional sea chanty, "What can you do
with a drunken sailor?")

# Death Disrupts Us

Death disrupts us
Breaks us from habit, ruins routines
Reminds us:
We are both eternal
and not.

Are the dead buried when the burial's done?
Do our parting sorrows replace prayer?
Is there a way -- beyond belief --
To  keep this going,
    to breathe beyond grief?

Death returns us to innocence
Back to our original contact with the world.
In our fragile, tender selves
    we sail, again,
        as we did the last time:
            survivors.

Death takes away our comfort.
It is where, finally, even words fail us.
And since there is no viable option
    we go on.

# Vacation with Cat

The cat, who is old and neutered and
has had multiple strokes and is deaf
and declawed and walks sideways
sits curled up beside me
on the stoop.

He's a badass: Takes on raccoons
and dominates the neighborhood
and the ladies are in awe.
He has an attitude and
you have to admire him --
He expects no quarter and gives none.
Named after the beer, Bud
creates his own climate.

I too am old. I don't dominate
(though there have been moments).
Right now the women are gone and I have
The house, the stoop, the life and the cat to myself.

This freedom to schedule the day is good --
no control, with a whim to guide the way --
Like being a boy when the world was
more than could be imagined
more than a day could hold
more than a cat.

Tomorrow I will do some work
and check off the chores left for me
and drink a little and do what I please
and read and smoke and put up my feet.

But right now, Bud wants to eat.

# Sweeping

An old woman in an apron
in an old black and white picture
is sweeping her steps.
Down the street from her
another woman is doing the same
and down from her, another.

Across my street, the good looking young woman
comes out in full technicolor
and begins sweeping her steps.
She is wearing shorts and her motion is like waves
beach-breaking on a calm day:
back and forth, rhythmic, repetitive.
The broom in her hand feels hard
as she pushes it in wide strokes and short ones,
roughly caressing surfaces, jabbing quickly into corners.
She goes over and over where she went before.
She is painting, day-dreaming as much as cleaning.

Up the street the old guy is more brisk.
He uses his broom like a weapon
efficiently clearing first his steps,
then his walkway, then the sidewalk.
He is fussy.  If he could, he would
sweep out into the street, around the corner
down to the shops, onto the highway
and out to the world.
We would never see him again.

When the neighbors moved in twenty years ago
my daughter, then age four,
full of blond-headed, sun-bright energy,
watched entranced for a while then went out to the garage
and came back with a broom twice her size.
She walked over and asked
if they needed any sweeping done.

It is not love that makes the world go round,
Not money or the moon or magnetism or power.
It is not history repeating, or oceans warming and cooling.
It is,
simply,
sweeping.

## Elissa Cottle

*I write poetry for my health. I start to feel not well if I haven't written a poem after a period of time. Poetry helps me stay in relationship with God and with myself.*

*Linden Hills gives me a home to make, a place to buy food without nitrites for my family, and a place for deep friendship with a few special people. It's a place that lets me practice the art of gratefulness without doctrine.*

# To Harriet

The lake took me back this year,
and how could she resist?
I offered her my second born and she gushed
at the sight of him.
Brown eyes bigger than islands,
he went in over his head
lashes wet and willing
to go in again.

The night after
I thanked her
with my own body.
In the dark, clothes dropped
on the cool sand,
I walked in, breasts
swelling in their own
warm and generous water.

# Permission to Write

You may take the rest of your life to write.
You may put everything beside it.
You may think about writing when you wake,
talk business of the day, lie down, make love, the writing
may be with you, beside anyone else who's there.
Every interaction may be examined.
Each person may be peeled, diced and reconstituted
into metaphor. You may metaphor yourself, part by part,
in each angle of the sun as it rises and sets.
You may let things grow as they may, grass, trees,
violets, dandelions. You may gently tell the house painter
he will cut your ivy over your dead body.
You may instruct him to paint carefully under those vines
clinging to your house. You may talk from your heart,
even to people who don't speak that language.
You may teach that language to those
who are not native speakers of the heart.
It is your first language.

# *Esam Aal*

*I've found I can put my thoughts, sentiments and reflections into poetry easier and more concisely than in other kinds of writing. I'm more of a sprinter than a long distance runner when it comes to writing.*

*We moved to Linden Hills in 1975 when we found an affordable house that was close to my wife's best friend, who happened to be married to my best friend. The allure of the neighborhood became clear later.*

## Blinded by the Rage

Blinded by the heat

See no light

Wounded and free

Helter skelter

The Guillotine has new minders now

Reason will have to wait

God is on our side

My law is his

Get the enemy

Get the infidels

# Shrouding

"We are not Jesus,"
We are Muslim," barked the teacher at Sunday school.
Samia, the startled little girl, now in her twenties,
is donning a hijab
An extensive one
No hair showing
Head and ears fully concealed
A solid shield
Fending heathen thoughts.
"Who, otherwise would marry you," warned her mother
"Make-up and Jeans are not for us,
It is for them."

"They love life," said El Imam
How dare we question him?
"Assalam Alikum," mumbled Samia.
Now wrapped in a white shroud-like garb
Body-shape must be concealed
Following her little brother
Her chaperon.

Freedom is for them
They are not like us
"They love life."

# Marhaban

Shortly before September 11,
A sign hung over a house gate
The sign said, "Welcome"
In Arabic.
"Marhaban" was scribbled on brown cardboard
Unremarkable
The author, an Arab, I presume
Likely Muslim.

Approaching his house now on my nightly walks
I never fail to notice
The absence of the sign.

# Sam Wilhide

*I didn't really choose to be a poet. It was kind of a family curse, like alcoholism or being a werewolf. One day I wrote a poem for my pet bird. The next day I wrote a poem for a girl I liked, comparing her to her favorite brand of snack pretzels.*

*I soon realized that I wasn't alone. Poetry had overflowed the levees and swamped the poorest neighborhoods of the city. There was a shortage of paper, so the poor kids wrote poetry on the necks of the math club. My poetry developed separately, mostly untouched by the currents of rap, slam or spoken word. Linden Hills was the dry land from which I was able to launch my poetic career. It was also, however, something like an island.*

# So much for the home security system

The squirrels took Ronald yesterday.

They snuck up on him

as he lay

inside his cozy quilt cocoon

(It was a chilly night in June).

They squeezed him through

the window pane,

whooping and shouting

and chanting his name

beneath the sleepless moon.

# I Am the Dandelion

I am the dandelion,
The weed.
Ain't no garden on Earth
Safe from me.
I am the dandelion,
I can grow
On the side of cliffs
And even in the hardest
City sidewalks.
I am the dandelion,
You can cut me
And burn me
And trample me into the ground,
But my roots go deeper
Than you'll ever know
And you can bet your sweet ass
I'll be here next spring
With my smilin' yellow flowers
In your face.

# Earwax

Earwax is the only thing standing between us
But every day there's more of it.

That's why I'm so slow to answer your questions
Of demanding relationship significance.

That's why, when you slip your tongue in my ear,
After whispering which Socratic dialogue

We should perform that night in the nude,
You stick to me and have to struggle to get yourself loose.

They say that the brain is the biggest erogenous zone
But the ear is close, and easier to lick.

I wouldn't let you lick my brain anyway,
You might rekindle old, long repressed memories -

Like the time I was suckled by a she-wolf at the zoo,
Or when my brother leaped my battlements
   and I awkwardly grabbed his penis.

If earwax was made of olive oil you could dip
Your bread in it, or shake it on your salad.

As it is we're at an impasse,
And your voice becomes more distant every day.

## Papier Mache

I'm a paper man, a man on paper
a piece of old news blowing down the street
I'm an inky slice, a scribbled sheet
a ball of crumpled up dreams.

Yeh, I'm a paper boy, the boy on paper
The shadow of a thousand signatures
I'm a phone number, a bad picture
a stack of forgotten reams.

Man, I'm the paper paper paper man
the torn up paper airplane wing
the careful little paper crane
a love letter lost in the mail.

I'm the paper moon and the cardboard sun
With a Xerox you can copy me
And when I'm written off I'll be
Just what I've written down.

# Felicity Britton

*I write poetry as an emotional release. I'm much better at communicating through the written word than verbally. I like the thoughtfulness of poetry, the fact that you have to spend time crafting a line, rather than speaking off the top of your head.*

*My relationship to Linden Hills is that of a grateful lodger. I feel so blessed to live among these people, these old trees, the park, the shops, close to the schools. I really do feel like I live in a small village, where people know my family and look out for us.*

42

# First Snow

I'm driving in December.
Slowly, carefully -
At life speed for a change.
I see three huskies hauling their owners
over unshovelled sidewalks.
They're so at home today
Excited to see the snow, gamboling in their joy.

Further on I see a grandma holding a baby
While mom and dad adjust his hat.
He's pulled it off twice before I pass.

And I wonder where I lie on that time line
Between ecstasy and non-acceptance.
My kids sledding outside with their dad,
While I run errands instead.
Two thirds of my life spent on a tropical island,
One third in this winter wonderland.
And I decide where you lie
Depends on where you call home.

# North Sydney, 7:28PM

Taxis cruise like sharks,
Gray against the rain slicked streets.
I'm sitting at the window
of a restaurant in Walker St.
Picking at my food
wishing I was alone.
Wishing one of those sharks
would suck me in
swallow me whole
and take me home.

# Sunday, August 27

You pulled me up when I was drowning
Put me on your back and swam
Set me gently on the seashore
Made sure I was whole again.
Held me close to hear my heart beat
Helped me, nursed me back to strength
Breathed your life into my body
Gazed into my eyes at length
Looked inside my soul and loved me
Even though you saw my flaws.

Yet I have nothing I can give you
Save my love and my applause.
I can't give you wealth or riches
I don't have material things
But if you're ever lost or drowning
I'll put you on my back and swim.

# Water Music

We prided ourselves on being different;
Loving, living, seeing different.
No time for explanations.
Surrealists.
But now our scene
Is a watercolour.
We are mere smudges
Of colour on our page.
Laughter and music,
Vaguely distant
Remind me of a memory
Or perhaps a forgotten dream.

I ask you did I ever lie
Was I never loyal?
But the music changes
And the moment is gone.
Was I not a friend?
Or merely a child?
Have we changed
Along with the music –
It gets increasingly distant
And the scene
Is more water than colour
As I kiss you
Goodbye.

# Demons

When you're not here,
flying mouths with hungry teeth
and fiery tails devour me
until once more you're near.

When you're not around
Ravenous wolves with mournful howls
snap and snarl and hunt me down
until once more I am found.

But when you're here, on your return
the dark clouds part, the sun shines bright
I melt in you and feel love's burn.

# Sally's Song

Pinstripe suit or leather jacket
I want a man who earns a packet
Gucci shoes, belt buckle and tie
and dollar signs in each blue eye
Leather briefcase, stocks and shares
When he I find, I'll have no cares
Mercedes, Lexus or a Jag would do,
I'd even settle for an Alfa or two.
Architect or merchant banker
(I don't want a common wanker)
*I want a yuppie, yes a yuppie*

If you won't shower with me,
Shower me with
Diamonds and furs
And those sorts of gifts
You know I want money
I don't want to earn it
Just let me have it,
I surely won't burn it.
Trust me I'll say
I'm not marrying for bills
I just won't say "I do"
Till I'm left in your will
*I want a yuppie, yes a yuppie*

I want a man with a house

With waterfront views

Who listens to "Finance"

On the 6 o'clock news.

An office in the city

He'd leave about seven

I'd be there on his desk

To have sex at eleven

Country clubs and second homes

Now why can't you see

That the ultimate accessory

Is sweet little me...

*I want a yuppie, yes a yuppie*

*Not a puppy or a guppy*

*Just a yuppie*

# My daughter likes pesto the best-o.

She has it on chicken,
She has it on lamb,
She has it on meatloaf
And roast beef and ham.

She has it with pasta
And parmesan cheese
She likes it on corn
and carrots and peas.

She has it with pizza,
She smears it on bread
And because she is two
She has some on her head

She has it on pork chops
and lamb chops and stew
If you were garlic and basil
Then she'd eat you too.

She has it on lasagna
Alfredo and toast
She doesn't like many foods
But she likes this food the most.

Some might say she's repetitive
Even obsessed-o
I'd have to agree
When it comes to her pesto.

50

## Stephan GrandPré

*I have been writing poetry since eighth grade. I started because I liked it and kept doing it to express myself.*

*I've lived in Linden Hills for 21 years and love the place. Aside from my family, I was raised at the library, Butler Drug, Tom Thumb and Creative Kidstuff... and, of course, Lake Harriet.*

# God's Face

If the dark sky is God's face...
The stars are his eyes
Glistening reflections of the ocean's waves
Twinkling with the sound of white tides

Shooting stars could be God rolling His eyes
Perhaps at our mistakes or our mistaken thoughts
Or maybe He's winking
To remind us of the joy, love, and beauty He's brought

The soft breeze is God's goodnight kiss
And the thunder tucks us in
The Northern lights are the blush on His cheeks
As He sees how amazing all of His children are

When the clouds are thick and the stars are hidden
Is God dreaming?
What is He dreaming about?
The future? The past?  Does God have nightmares?

Or maybe the starless sky means He's praying
Does God pray for us? To us?
Does God pray for Himself?
Does he thank us in his prayers?

The morning dew could be God's sweat, or tears
Does God cry when He dreams?
Does He cry when He prays?
Are they tears of joy?

# He Squints to See the Stars

He squints to see the stars
I mean, he takes off his glasses
Raises his face to the moon
And he squints to see the stars

He's done it for years
But tonight was different
Tonight he took his glasses off
And he looked at the stars

He didn't squint this time
He simply opened his eyes
Opened them as wide as he could
Tonight he saw more than he's ever seen

He saw the most beautiful thing
The sky danced before him
It was no longer night
But the most gorgeous canvas he had ever pondered

Tonight he didn't squint
All he did was open his eyes
It was raining and clouds filled the sky
Yet nobody told him what he saw

If he had known he might have fainted
Because beauty is beauty
It doesn't matter what it is
Beauty is beauty, no matter how the sky is painted.

## She thinks I'm a good story teller

I don't know if this is a story
Not sure if it's poetry
But I hope I can tell it right
    I miss her because...
    Textbooks don't laugh at my jokes,
    Or for no reason at all.
    Because my professors aren't happy to see me
    in the morning.
    Wouldn't care for a hug from them anyways,
    And I don't see the care in their eyes.


Does she know how I fell?
I can't tell
    I miss her 'cause my roommates can't find comfort
      in the silence between us.
    Her still lips are just as precious as the words spoken
    And my late night conversations are less fulfilling
    When they're with Sports Center, CNN, and
      other pixilated companions.
    ESPN doesn't play cribbage.


It's strange loving someone who...
I can't tell
    I miss her because her voice isn't the same
    Without her smile
    I roll over too freely
    I can't hold down two pillows on my own,
    Because the balled up comforter I hold while I dream is cold
    And never squeezes back.

Maybe this is a story
That I can't tell
  I miss her because I hit the snooze so I can sleep later
  Instead of laying next to her longer
  Watching her and wondering
  What she might be dreaming.

Is she dreaming of me right now?
I can't tell
  I miss her because the sunrise doesn't shine
  into my eyes
  Off the face of my pillow.
  It's not so much that I miss looking at her
  It's that I miss her looking at me
  Because her eyes are so...
  Just like she is.

People tell me that I've got something special,
But I tell them, "That's who I've been missing."

# Saturday's a Rugby Day

Taking the frosted pitch early on a late autumn
Saturday morning
The wind blows the makeshift goalposts shakily
back and forth
My comrades, still dazed by the night before,
Smell like stale beer and lost memories
Dirtier than they will be after this eighty minute war

We are soldiers
Fifteen men clash
Face to face
Fist to face
Knee to face
With fifteen men for eighty minutes

Soldiers of the ruck and the scrum, the maul and the pitch
Men standing in the sobering cold on thawing grass
Exposing bare skin, bruised knees, chapped hands,
bloodied faces
Each man in his kit
From cleat to mouth guard
Feeling older than his days
Preparing to make other men feel even older on Sunday.

The battles so routine
Far from the rehearsals of practice
Bullets of tackles
Grenades of hits
Landmines of cheap shots.

Bodies are waking

Stiff muscles and cracking joints

Limping strides and slowly focusing minds

All awaiting the cry of war

Translated to the boom of boot striking ball

The kick off soars high

Scraping the overcast

The sound of it muffled

Representing the beginning

Harsh and hard, bloody and wet

Cold and muddy, painful and consented

The beginning of a war

The beginning of eighty minutes.

# George Scott

*I like to fiddle with words and the way they fit together to form phrases and sentences, then see how those can be developed into a metrical flow of thought. For me, rhyming lines are like getting Green Stamps on your purchase -- a little something extra. Writing poetry also gives me a politically correct way to be rowdy, raucous and blasphemous.*

*We moved to Linden Hills more by chance than by choice. We liked the area and, especially when the kids were in school, stuff was handy and we didn't need a car to go where we wanted to. Now we stay mostly because we're too damn lazy to move.*

# The Limerick

Dirges and sonnets, 'tis true
Reflect topics of most somber hue.
If you like twisted logic
Or themes scatalogic
Then limerick's the verse form for you.

A limericker has no compunctions
About dealing with bodily functions
Or putting wry faces
On all human races
In spite of our modern injunctions.

So if your limerick is bawdily tinted
Or you've some new blasphemy minted
You'd best write it on
The wall of some john
Or else it will never get printed.

## Snowfall

With ten inches of snow one despairs;
It covers our sidewalks and stairs
And, wouldn't you know
We got this big snow
While our snowblower's in for repairs.

## The Perfect Man

A lusty young widow, Ms. Fenchers
Sought a man to share life's adventures.
She found one ere long
But she knew he was wrong
When her kisses blew out his dentures.

## Cat Hunting

A city-bred nimrod named Bards
Hunted game with his cat in back yards.
It would stalk and would flush
With a great feline rush
But retrieving was not in the cards.

## Reunions

Class reunions get harder to bear,
What with hearing aids and grey hair
It's hard for this youth
To face the sad truth
That I'm one of the old people there.

# Bad Smoke

A careless old doper named Strong
Let his face hair grow nine inches long
Then he had a big fright
As it burned off one night
When he took a big hit from his bong.

# Fantasy

A horny young freshman named Borts
Would ogle the girls in short shorts.
A miniscule halter
Would make his heart falter
As he dreamed of non-vertical sports.

But then in his room in the dorm
On a night exceedingly warm
A girl most delicious
Agreed to his wishes
Upon which he couldn't perform.

# Schoolboy's Lament

Here it is, the last of May,
You can smell that summer's coming.
The apple trees have budded out
And bees are really humming.

The farmers are done plowing the ground;
They've shed their disks and their harrows.
The machinery will sit 'till early next fall
And make like roosts for the sparrows.

My long-handled drawers are stored away, too:
They're itchy to wear in the heat.
My shoes and socks will stay under the bed --
Summer's the time for bare feet.

When summertime comes, though, you've got to look out.
Poison ivy and ticks can be cruel.
Still I'd rather look out for things such as those
Than look out a window at school.

# A Pessimist's Ode to Spring

I was looking for March winds
To banish winter's blues
But all we got was gloppy slush
That crudded up my shoes.

I hoped that April showers
Would make planting not so hard,
But what we got was flooding rains
That washed away my yard.

Now May should bring bright flowers:
That's what the old poem said.
But based on what I've seen so far
We'll just get weeds instead.

I plan to use the lessons
From what I've so far seen.
I plan to pave my whole darned yard
With asphalt painted green.

# Breezes

The morning breezes are blowing
As I leisurely sit here and scrub.
The bubbles that burst on the surface
Waft tellingly over the tub.

The afternoon breezes are blowing
Helped by a small ceiling fan.
They rise to fill up the nostrils
Just after I rise from the can.

The breezes of evening are blowing
As I snooze in my old easy chair.
The sounds and scents of my slumber
Let everyone know I am there.

The breezes of night time are blowing
At a time when we should be lovers.
The side effects of my efforts
Ruffle both her and the covers.

If the breezes don't stop their blowing
She's headed for Vegas or Reno.
I could stop this pending departure
Simply by taking some Beano.

These breezes, to me, are a comfort,
An activity at which I am deft.
At my age, with most functions failing,
It's one of the few I have left.

So Beano is out of the question
And I guess I'll keep breezing alone
And smile when I create the breezes:
At least I'll be sure they're my own.

# Happy Hour

At a bar one rainy evening
When half the drinks were free,
A guy came in, then asked for gin
And took the stool right next to me.

"How have you been?" he asked me.
I said that I'm doing good.
"Me too, so far," then he rapped on the bar
"But I've got to keep tapping on wood."

"Remember? My wife was to leave me
And I was about to give in.
Then I met a new love, gave my first wife the shove,
Now I'm happier than I've ever been."

We talked about personal matters
And exchanged our ideas on sex.
He asked after my folks, we swapped a few jokes,
Then he picked up both of our checks.

He said he'd enjoyed being with me
And smiled as he waved a goodbye.
I asked the bartender, but he couldn't remember:
Just who in the hell was that guy?

# Progression

While making conversation
Two find a common theme
And then they find a common mind
That melts into a dream.

Whispers in the darkness
Speak words of sweet desire;
One may be bold, the other cold:
It takes two to light a fire.

Physical attraction
Outweighs the waiting game.
When the time is right, one steamy night
Love bursts into flame.

Relationship develops
And finds a common goal;
In quiet fashion they find that passion
Plays a gentler role.

Time then alters ardor
To companionship – as sweet.
Their courtship done they act as one
And find their love complete.

# Jolene Gustafson

*I write poetry because it's the best way for me to make sense of the world and it is just something I seem to need to do. I've dabbled in it since I was a young child and studied it in graduate school and writing workshops.*

*When I visited Minnesota at Christmas my sister and brother-in-law took my daughter and me sledding at Beards Plaisance, browsing at the Wild Rumpus, and out to eat at Rice Paper. Not surprisingly, we fell in love with the neighborhood. When I saw a house in my price range, I put an offer on it from Maryland without ever having stepped inside.*

# Needles

"A woman enters a hospital with chest pains
and doctors find a needle in her heart,"
states the morning radio d.j.—
not the opening to a joke
but a news story.
I hear this in the back of a cab.

The d.j. and his sidekick muse
about her clutziness.
I wonder about the delayed pain;
about the condition of a heart
that doesn't register a sharp object
until days after its entry.

Throughout a long workday, her
metallic heart enters my thoughts
in irregular stitches. By four,
I'm full of questions—about how
her heart grew numb,
if there were warning signs.

As the day runs on, I think about her
less. In fact, I've nearly forgotten the needle
woman by the time I thread myself into another cab
too tired for the walk and metro ride
to the train that will finally get me home.
The cab driver sings an airy, Spanish song,
and I wish we were in his bed. Wish he was singing
me and our child to sleep.

# Midnight Sestina

Around your neck you've wrapped a scarf,
with Aztec birds in a row like letters
that spell out a sentence, or like the weeks
that run across my calendar.
It's easier to look at the scarf than at your face,
which has those eyes that are dark as midnight.

But in my dreams, the ones borne of midnight,
it is your eyes that I see—not the scarf.
At night it no longer shadows your face.
During waking hours, I write you letters
that are never mailed. I stack them near my calendar
using them to count how many weeks

I've been enamored of you. Weak's
my normal state these days—thank God, midnight
is different. In dreams, I walk to my calendar,
collect the stack, and offer it to you for your scarf.
Those 12 Aztec birds, for me, are the letters
that spell your name. I love them like your face.

Time has become a Dali painting—clock face
melting over my days, disguising the weeks
wasted away. I write for a living, but love letters
won't pay for a warm resting spot at midnight.
Nor can I wrap my tired limbs in your scarf
to chase chills away. I have only a flimsy calendar

70

to sustain my peaceful nights. But no calendar
is sturdy enough to lift my face
at dawn. Sunlight arrives: a wild dog set to scarf
any remaining morsels of strength. As the weeks
begin to blur—lemon yellow sliding to midnight
blue—my alphabet dwindles to 12 letters.

So I turn to others, writers of *belles lettres,*
to guide me away from the metal calendar
that presses my lucidity between midnight
sheets. I want to study your face
under the sun's spotlight in coming weeks
and to hold in my hands your scarf.

I'll pluck the Aztec birds for my watch face
and change my calendar's months and weeks,
renaming *March* midnight and *Sunday* scarf.

# Lessons with My Great Aunt Elsie

I can't remember hearing your voice
read tales of princesses lying in wait.
But I do recall feeling the heroine
wrapped in your fortress arms, content
to listen to endless rounds
of "You Are My Sunshine."
Being four years old, I believed
your notes were what made my hair golden.

I remember when you tried to teach me Swedish.
You wrote each word in a small, spiral notebook
stored in your kitchen drawer. I remember
*God Jul* (Merry Christmas)
*min svenska flicka* (my Swedish girl)
*sjunga* (sing)
*vinter* (winter).

Standing at your grave that January morning
I believed my grief had altered the weather.
Your serenade served as a perverse soundtrack.
Under a cement-gray sky, with winds dropping
the temperature to minus 75, I held
a single pomegranate-red rose under my coat.
My family huddled around me, trying to stop
the icy blades that sliced through to my core.

Suddenly I knew how Demeter must have felt
as she searched the meadows near Eleusis,
too late to halt her child's abduction. I knew
the rage that made her punish the world
with the chilling winds of winter
and skies too angry to return
anything, even snow.

# Briars and Roses

She travels backwards through the darkness,
over the guard dogs, prostrate by the door,
who've lain down without circling their beds;

past the rooms of dreamless sleepers;
out into the yard, where the birds continue
planting briars, rows deep, around the stone walls.

She can smell the garden through the latticework
of branches—the new roses and the damp
back of the man who tends them.

If she could once again taste
his salty skin, she would break
from the hourglass of movement
that funnels her from her bed to this spot
and back.

Her hair, thick as vines,
gleams in the room void of light,
where not even the moon is allowed
to approach her bed; the incandescence of dreams
filtering out each strand, growing stronger

each year she's made to sleep alone.

# Carrie Bassett

*I write poetry because I need to say things, and I need to say them right, that is, in a way that goes—zing!—to the essence of the idea, feeling, emotion, experience. Recollected in tranquility (and worked at in my notebook and on my computer), the poem grows, shifts, morphs, and sometimes disappears altogether. Never is it at the end what I thought it would be when I began.*

*Linden Hills snuggles up to Lake Harriet, the center of the universe for me. From here the lake is more accessible and friendly than on the other shores. Linden Hills is cozy, convenient, and compatible.*

# Many Loves

I have had many loves.

The fireman took me up ladders into fiery buildings
and we jumped many floors
into the held hoop waiting below.

The accountant spoke numbers to me
and taught me FIFO
      First in, first out
and LIFO
      Last in, first out
and balance sheets.
I was in the black with him
But he in the red for me—
I couldn't understand (497).

And there were several professors,
one of physics who found my center of gravity
but had too much gravitas,
another of psychology who manipulated my mind
but left my body untouched.

The carpenter took my measurements and built me up.
The contractor tore me down.

But the poet spoke Neruda:

       "My happiness bites the plum of your mouth."

He spoke Rumi and Kabir—

       about the rain bird dying of thirst,

       who refuses all water but the rain.

Like Emily Dickinson, he told all the truth,

but he told it slant.


Only the poet did with me "what the spring does

       to the cherry tree."

He made my blood bloom and my soul stand up and shout—

and then weep when he left, taking

his words with him.

# Tanguera

If wisdom was a woman, she would be a tanguera.
She would dance the tango—wildly, ferociously, passionately.
Quietly, demurely.

When she follows the man's lead,
    her feminist hackles do not rise.
That's because she knows—and I do not—
    that it's a conversation, that he needs her too,
that he invites and indicates and she chooses.
She can respond minimally or with ornaments,
    flicking her legs with amagues or beveling her ankles.

She knows—as I don't—the strength of the stance
    of being collected, feet together,
    weight on one leg, waiting
    for the invitation or the next move—back perhaps
    or forward diagonally into an ocho, a turn.

She knows, as I am learning, that her job,
    once the step has been taken,
    is to return to centered balance,
    the *kamal* point from which all is possible.

She knows—as I am far from understanding—

       that the universal cadence is manifesting here,

in her and in her partner,

of turbulence and return to equilibrium, like breath, like tides.


She knows—and I feel sometimes—that $1+1+1 = 1$:

my partner, the music, and I are one.


       She knows how—I only know what.

# Kirsten Bergh

*Kirsten's poetry inspired and held me when she died so suddenly. I found comfort, inspiration, compassion and hope. I continue to be grateful for her poems, for they not only helped to heal me and others, but they keep her spirit alive. Her book has touched many people she never met. This means a great deal to me as a mother.*

*Kirsten loved living in Linden Hills. She worked at the Co-op, played in the park and babysat for kids in the neighborhood. In both casual and profound ways she "claimed" this place as her home.*

*-- Linda Bergh*

# Reading You

I would like to scream
like a siren at you
But I won't, 'cause
I know what you
would do.  See, I can
read you like a book,
sometimes.  Yeah, and we
got the same battle
tactics, the same escape
plans.  So I might as
well scream at me.

Sometimes I forget to
read between your lines
and I lose my place
though I try to
remember to fold down
the corners when I stop
reading.  And sometimes
you're just you and
there's no me reflecting
and that's when I gotta
get out my dictionary.

# Just Paul and Me

And then it's just
Me and Paul
And the night
Him just crooning
About playgrounds
And women
And nonsense
With a scratchy
Old record sound
And me just
Twirling
With my reflection
Like some
Fancy-dancy
Make-believe queen
Dancing the polka

And the night
Just sitting there
Staring at us
As if we were crazy
Or something.
I guess we are
Because I'm all alone
Just me
And my reflection.

Put that in one of
Your songs, Paul:
A crazy girl
Dancing with her
Shadow
Because there's
No one else left
For her
To dance with.

# Mannequin Moon

Sometimes the moon gets lost
In the city, among the globes
glowing fluorescent
Strung like onions
Along the spines of the bridges,
Among the drooping streetlights,
Behind the square office eyes,
The pale boxy teeth, grinning like
An unfinished scrabble game
On the looming black blocks of buildings
Posed like dominoes.

But you might find it
Gleaming from an upstairs window
Like a light left on
Glowing like mercury
In a shadowed-alley puddle,
Or peeping like a frightened face
Pale and timid
From behind the sharp crack
Of a blackened corner wall,
Or maybe shining double
Like car headlights
In the useless glasses
Of a mannequin in a
Glass shop window,
Rounded and white
Like polished pebbles.

# The Sun Is Shining

The sun is shining
the sky is blue
Shall we go out
in the world today?
The air is sweet
the day is new
Adventure is only
a footstep away.

There are drums to be played
There are bells to be rung
There are thousands of
Heart-lifting songs to be sung.

Shall we ring them?
Shall we sing them?
To the beat of the drum?

# Footprints

We strolled along the beach together
The ocean and I.
She fingered the shiny pebbles
That I let drop.
She filled my wandering footsteps
With her own watery feet
Leaving subtle valleys
Glazed with silver
On the sand.

We played tag
The ocean and I.
She burbled when she caught me,
tickling my toes
With tentative fingers.
She reached into her
Deep shadowy pockets
And tossed out creamy shells
Onto the sand
For me to gather.

We spoke of many things
The ocean and I.
She whispered to me
Tales of faraway lands
With castles high on hilltops green,
Of crystal beaches
And golden suns.

I talked to her of sneakers
And of marbles.
And of how pretty a daisy looks
When it dances in the wind.
I collapsed on the sand
And listened to the ocean
Sing me her lullaby.

And when the evening descended
We watched the sun go down
Together, the ocean and I.

# For You, Papa

I thought I heard your footsteps
running toward me, disturbing the stones
But when I opened my eyes
I saw it was only the waves
pulling and swirling like hands.

I thought I felt your smile,
warm and loving upon my face
But when I opened my eyes
I saw it was only the sun
beaming at me from across the water.

I thought I heard you
whisper my name
But when I opened my eyes
I realized it was only the wind
playing in my hair.

I thought I felt you
softly kiss my cheek
But when I opened my eyes
I saw it was only a leaf
caressing me with gentle strokes.

And then I felt your love
in and all around me
Powerful, yet gentle like the waves,
Warm and shining like the sun,
Soft yet strong like the wind,
Tender and alive like the leaves.

And I didn't even have to open my eyes:
I knew you were there.

# Up Here

From up here
you are very little
Not less important
just easier to deal with
and harder to love,
like a stranger.

Up here I am queen of myself
and follow no one's rule
but my own.
I am the chosen
the Maker-of-Decisions.
I decide when to laugh
and when to frown
what to think
and when to love.

Up here I piss when I want to piss
I am untouched by rejection
anger and fear
by all save
the sun, the rain, the wind
and the rocks beneath my feet.

Up here I am always beautiful
always free --

And up here
I am always alone.

90

# Rocks

his words fell
like rocks from his mouth
and clattered all around him.
even after
the avalanche had cleared
I could feel them jostling
around
in my head
keeping me awake.

# Ask

Would you come
if I asked
and hold my hand
and walk with me
barefoot
over long, wet meadow grass
under the moon?

Would you lie close to me
if I asked
and keep me warm
in your arms
and laugh with me
under the starlight?

Would you tell me
if I asked
of the dreams of your heart
and trust me with your tears
as we walk through the woods
under the rain?

Would you sing with me
in harmony
if I asked
and dream with me
of castles and somedays
as we sit and swing like children
under the haloing branches of the trees?

Would you dance with me
in the starlight
if I asked
and kiss me without shame
and smile at me with your eyes?

Would you love me
simply and openly
like a flower
if I were to ask?

And would you anyway
even if I didn't?

## To Nina and Me

When we're grandmas together
Maybe we'll be soft and beautiful like clouds
And sweet and rosy with laughter like apples
And we'll be free and graceful

Like the summer grasses
Of our barefoot youth.
Maybe you'll still have dimples
Curled up like two fetuses in your cheeks
Creased with countless smiles and births

And maybe there still will be
Freckles scattered across my nose
Like the huts of an African village in the heat
Hiding in the wrinkles that gather at my eyes
Like animals around a watering hole.

And we'll tell our wide-eyed grandbabies
About iced-grapefruit chapstick.

# Cristopher Anderson

*I just love writing poetry and it seems to give me a way to participate directly in an art form.*

*We were originally drawn to Linden Hills because of the neighborhood's charm and quirky people. We like being near the food co-op and the library as well as having the lakes close for walks, cross-country skiing, boating and swimming. We appreciate the civic, cultural and artistic depth of our friends and neighbors.*

# Smile

Ah, – her garden plant smell,
fruity breath and flashing eyes!

This morning light bright on the river smile.

Memory of our courtship dance of
trembling and heat.

This other half of everything
      settling into my arms.

# Cat

When you live with a cat whose
grandfather came from an Asian jungle,
you don't expect much purring.

A jump on your stomach – "Yes,
you can pet me now.  Once is enough.
isn't it time to eat?"

You watch her.
For a long time.

When a muscle moves
something inside of you
comes alive!

# Dragonfly

The boy says he loves
dragonflies – elegant and
earnest; that dragonfly esprit.

He follows in the slipstream
behind his uncle down to the water's edge,
watching the man's hands on
rope and board, readying the boat.

He knows he's going somewhere.
He looks at his own small hands.

Inside his body, little hesitations
have come to live like small animals.
And what he thought was easy is now near
cliff and rock, with the sea crashing and racing.

He searches the eyes of this man,
looking for something alive, some way
through this heaving of desire and fear.

The man says he knows this boy.

# How the Lover

How the lover wears her hair, or
the shape of her skirt or when her fingers move;
His hickory tree breath, timbre of voice,
how his eyes gently pierce – all this is decided.

He or she is it, and
what matters is the river flowing between,
slipping the lovers off their feet into
currents of wanting and being wanted.

The school for this is the father arching his brow and smiling,
the mother relaxing and loosening her arms,
the girl or boy laughing into the laughing faces of friends.

The young one strides confidently into our midst
carrying in her arms the heart of the world –
and we gasp! We want to call out, "Please be careful!"
But, she is smiling and confident as she should be.

Shall we tell her our stories?

# My Uncle

My uncle, the genial criminal, cons Social Security checks from his aunt, molests his sister, burns the barn down for the money.

This is one story of Norwegians in America.

When he marries, he has girlfriends on the side. What he does to his daughters – my cousins – I don't know, but I see. He later makes a career of meeting widows.

And I loved him. He flew fighter planes during the good war, knew how to wear a top hat, told racy jokes and included me in his smile. He was famously loyal to his friend the alcoholic musician.

This is where I learned to be suspicious of love, my stomach tightening when he said, "Let me do something for you!"

But, I loved – one sad boy recognizing another.

# The Young Mother

The boy posing for the photo in the park with you and
the stone lion curls his lip and snarls with the biggest of them.

This is how these big cats can look
before our world gets to them.

And this brave heart is leaning into you and has your
arm around and tucking up against his ribs.

We see on your fore-finger the
dime store ring he has asked you to wear.

Oh my friend, the young mother –
Thank you for holding your son as you do.

Ready with your soft body, chalky musk of summer garden,
believing eyes that look and look and look.

We know how the cold rain will ache the bones.
And that, in the end, we must walk alone.

But this may be his warm wool coat.
And with you, dear woman – our trusting calm.

*-- For Marisha*

# The Poet Apologizes

The poet apologizes for his absence.
A few months have gone by and he
says, "I sometimes do this."

We grin.
We know about this loneliness –

This turning toward the lost father,
forgotten lover,
the shame of children.

So the coffee goes stale and the cupboard empties?

This morning, he's with the spider as
she's mending her nets from the
bugs brought in during the night.

It's not pretty. She's not pretty and neither is he.

But now we have these juicy little words
that serve so well, touching
this ache.

-- *For Thomas*

# Summer Insects

There are summer insects
who have just one wild night before
they leave as empty carapaces eddying down a stream,
their eggs left whirring and clicking near a rock.

They don't wonder about who they are or
why they're here or what's going to happen next.
They're busy twirling and tumbling and chasing each other
in some mad dance toward the stars.

They're not holding back.
They haven't learned to like the wrong things.
With them, it's this life and nothing else –
all splendid yearnings and delicious matings,
singing and dancing, eating and sometimes being eaten.

Fulfillment is simple destiny,
not a nagging question.
After the music, after the dance,
after the long sweet night
is a soft surrender, a
giving of oneself to the current
with others of my kind, so
some true pattern can be left
in the nature of things.

# Roses

Reading the newspaper one evening
we hear a laugh from the neighbor's garden.

Glancing up, we see they've both turned into roses –
David and Rita – cheeks reddened by drink and anticipation.

Something was just funny.
Their heads are ducking toward each other.
And they're smiling and swaying to the music.

We turn back to the news, thinking
we know all about desire, but then –
       We look back.

There he is, all on stem, poised and ready.
And there she is – twining red.
If we look away, we start to feel very lonely.

We notice them tilting toward each other –
He cocking his chin next to her ear and moving his sure feet.
She letting herself be held, breaking away,
then captured again.

What lovers do with each other is a private thing,
but all of the twilight garden is doing what it is doing.
And later, we see the moon taking her slow time
between the limbs of the tree.

The next morning –

we're watching again –

with their little table and napkins at breakfast,

he takes his chirpy grin and

juts his face toward her.


She notices,

lets her shoulders go, a

quiver moving down her stem.

The Poets of Linden Hills

## Esam Aal

... is a retired teacher. Originally from Egypt, he has written a memoir, "Leaving Egypt," as well as articles on Middle Eastern affairs. He landed in Minneapolis in 1969, just as Neil Armstrong was landing on the moon. He has a master's degree in counseling psychology and worked as a special teacher and horticulturalist. He is married (to Paula) and has two children, Kitty and Kareem. Kareem also writes poetry.

## Cristopher Anderson

... is an independent marketing and public relations professional. He's worked as a scene painter off-Broadway, sailed with the Danish Merchant Marine, tended bar and was a writer/producer/director with Prairie Public TV in North Dakota. His poetry has been published in regional journals and performed at local venues. He has also produced award-winning television journalism and documentary work that has aired on PBS. He is the founder and co-artistic director of Big Woods Transformational Theater. He is married to Maria Genné. They have two daughters.

## Carrie Bassett

... is the founder and director of The Wisdom Institute, which is a collaboration of independent thinkers interested in wisdom and useful ways of applying it in people's lives. She is also a faculty member at two distance learning universities as well as a board member of Theatre de la Jeune Lune. She is originally from Hoboken, NJ, and went to school across the street from where Frank Sinatra grew up. She is an award-winning Master Gardener and an ex-Peace Corps volunteer who taught English in Casablanca. She has two daughters.

108

**Kirsten Bergh**

... wrote poetry from the age of seven until she died in a tragic car accident at 17. Her father, Paul, died a year before that and her poetry reflects the struggles of a young woman coming of age in extraordinary circumstances. It's remarkable verse -- both for its clarity and emotional force and for its positive view of life. A book of her poetry and drawings, "She Would Draw Flowers," is in its fifth printing and has been used at weddings, funerals and performances, as well as in schools around the country.

**Felicity Britton**

... left the "sunny shores" of Australia to move to Minneapolis where she has become "a professional parent." She holds a B.A. in communications, has backpacked around Europe and worked as the marketing manager for a cruise line. She has written a romantic comedy and is working on a children's screenplay. She moved to Linden Hills 10 years ago after looking at 63 houses in the area. She is married to Bob Arnoldy and has two daughters, Isabelle and Lucinda.

**Elissa Cottle**

... is a homemaker, mother of two children and a creative writing teacher. She has published poems in several literary journals. She works as an editor and coordinator for neighborhood projects and holds a degree in journalism and political science from the University of Iowa. As a student, she attended youth music workshops and once conducted the Minnesota Orchestra in Schubert and Mozart symphonies. She chose Linden Hills as a good place to raise a family and has lived here for 15 years.

**Stephan GrandPré**

... is studying elementary education at the University of Wisconsin-River Falls. He hopes to become a teacher in Minneapolis. He plays intercollegiate rugby for UW-RF and is a devout college hockey fanatic. He's lived in "the yellow house on the corner" (of 43rd and Xerxes) almost all his life and worked at Linden Hills Park. He is a graduate of Clara Barton Open School and Minneapolis South High School.

**Jolene Gustafson**

... is a freelance writer and editor. She has worked on everything from educational web sites to museum materials to an Emmy award-winning children's series for the Discovery Channel. She received her degree in journalism from the University of Minnesota and has a master's degree in creative writing and publishing. She moved to Linden Hills in 2004 from the Baltimore-Washington area with her daughter, Isabel.

**George Scott**

... is retired from a career in advertising research and media planning. He's had poetry published in several magazines and newspapers. He likes to collect old phonograph records and go fishing. He and his wife, Clementine, have two grown sons and three grandchildren. He has lived in the same Linden Hills house since 1959, when he moved here after outgrowing a small house "in the slums of Edina."

**Doug Wilhide**

... is a writer, teacher and marketing communications consultant. He has worked as a copywriter and creative director at three Minneapolis advertising agencies and teaches graduate classes on advertising strategy at the University of St. Thomas College of Business. He holds degrees in English from Miami University (Ohio) and the University of Iowa. He moved to Linden Hills in 1983, just in time for two huge snow storms, temperatures in the minus-twenties, a furnace that quit and inlaws visiting for the holidays. He was appointed Poet Laureate of Linden Hills in 2004.

**Sam Wilhide**

... is taking classes at the University of Minnesota to become a math teacher. He graduated from the University of Wisconsin-Madison with a degree in philosophy and English, and taught for two years in Osaka, Japan. His poems and stories have won prizes and been published in various journals, newspapers and online. He attended Minneapolis South High School, where he was active in the theater program, playing Nathan Detroit in "Guys and Dolls." He is married to Jessica Beggiato of Cahors, France.

**Trolley Car Press**

is located in the Linden Hills area of Minneapolis.
Its mission is to publish and promote work that
reflects unique, individual perspectives and
enhances a sense of community.

For more information, or to order copies of
"Between the Lakes: The Poets of Linden Hills,"
please contact us.

Trolley Car Press

3019 West 43rd Street

Minneapolis, MN 55410

612.926.3939